~~Spring~~ #18
Freiheit

Cover: Romy Blümel

Inhalt

4	**VORWORT** Jule Hoffmann
9	**THE WALL** Doris Freigofas
31	**FREIHEIT – WIEDER NUR EIN GEFÜHL** marialuisa
47	**IN LIMBO** moki
53	**EH NICHTS PASSIERT** Stephanie Wunderlich
69	**DILE AADAM** Maren Amini
79	**O.T.** Carolin Löbbert
83	**IN DESPAIR** moki
95	**LET IT GROW** Moshtari Hilal
101	**DANCE!** Larissa Bertonasco
117	**AUFRAUSCHEN** Almuth Ertl
133	**MUST HAVE** Stephanie Wunderlich
137	**FREEDOM** Karina Tungari
157	**IN MY MIND** moki
165	**GANS IM GLÜCK** Katharina Kulenkampff
179	**O.T.** marialuisa
181	**INTO THE WILD** Carolin Löbbert
201	**O.T.** marialuisa
202	**ANZEIGEN**
219	**O.T.** marialuisa
220	**ZEICHNERINNEN**
225	**O.T.** Maren Amini
228	**ABOUT**

Ich ziehe meine Schuhe an, laufe die Treppen runter und lasse die Tür hinter mir ins Schloss fallen. Ich laufe los ohne nachzudenken, ohne Absichten, ohne Ziel. Alles, was eben noch wichtig war, lasse ich in der Wohnung zurück. Ein Gefühl der Leichtigkeit überkommt mich, wie wenn man nach einem langen Winter das erste Mal ohne Jacke auf die Straße geht. Ich kann jetzt tun und lassen, wonach mir ist. Mir einen Kaffee kaufen, Hunde und Menschen beobachten, Häuserfassaden betrachten, an denen ich tausend Mal achtlos vorbeigegangen bin, oder einfach nur gehen. Den Rhythmus der Schritte spüren, die Wärme, die in meinem Körper entsteht.

Auf belebten Straßen bin ich anonym. Ich kann alles sein und niemand. Der Spaziergang ist ein Freiraum, eine Flucht, ein Ausbruch aus allen funktionalen Zusammenhängen. Betont langsam schlendere ich an den Geschäften vorbei, am hektischen Verkehr, an Menschen, die Termine und Ziele verfolgen. Spazierend werde ich zur Außenseiterin, zur Aussteigerin. Mein zielloses Herumspazieren ist Arbeitsverweigerung, Kurzurlaub, eine Demonstration gegen das Effizienz-Diktat des Kapitalismus.

Diese Art von Spaziergang ist etwas völlig anderes als das verplauderte Spazieren zu zweit, das jetzt in der Pandemie der einzig verbliebene und schnell abgenutzte soziale Rahmen war. Er hat auch nichts zu tun mit dem banal-bürgerlichen Sonntagsspaziergang in der Natur. Ich spaziere alleine. Alleine zu gehen, kann radikale Freiheit bedeuten. Du kannst jedem deiner Impulse folgen. Du kannst dich selbst als Maßstab nehmen, nur auf deine eigenen Bedürfnisse achten. Du musst nicht rücksichtsvoll sein, nicht zurückhaltend, nicht vorsichtig, nicht leise, nicht empathisch, nicht höflich, nicht beschwichtigend, nicht hilfsbereit, nicht ausweichend. Ich nenne es den radikalen Spaziergang.

Als Frau alleine in der Öffentlichkeit sein zu können, ist eine Freiheit, die es zu verteidigen gilt. Gegen Sprüche, gegen Blicke, gegen die eigene Angst. In ihrem Buch »Wanderlust« beschreibt die US-amerikanische Schriftstellerin Rebecca Solnit, wie die Möglichkeit sexueller Gewalt implizit in Kommentaren, anzüglichen Blicken und Einschüchterungen schlummert und Frauen in ihrer Bewegungsfreiheit im öffentlichen Raum limitiert und beschneidet. Solnit beschreibt auch, wie im Europa des 19. Jahrhunderts Frauen, die sich ohne eindeutig identifizierbare Absichten auf der Straße bewegten, der Prostitution verdächtigt wurden. Alleine draußen unterwegs zu sein, wurde praktisch gleichgesetzt mit sexueller Verfügbarkeit. Das 19. Jahrhundert ist weit weg, aber etwas davon scheint übrig geblieben zu sein, oder warum fühle ich mich manchmal unwohl, wenn ich alleine am Badesee liege. Die Straße hat immer Männern gehört, und Frauen wurden in private Räume verwiesen, wo häusliche Aufgaben auf sie warteten. Klingt alles so nach 19. Jahrhundert, aber in der Coronakrise sind wieder vor allem Frauen in Teilzeit gegangen und haben zuhause die Betreuung der Kinder übernommen. Nach dem Motto: so haben wir das schon immer gemacht.

Der Zugriff auf den öffentlichen Raum, selbstbestimmt am Straßenleben teilzuhaben, sichtbar und unabhängig zu sein, und dabei mit niemandem reden zu müssen (oder eben auch mit allen reden zu können, ohne Angst davor zu haben, falsche Signale zu senden, sich als Beute zu gerieren), sollte für alle eine Grundfreiheit sein. Virginia Woolf hat in ihrem berühmten Essay »Ein Zimmer für sich allein« darüber geschrieben, wie wichtig nicht nur ökonomische Unabhängigkeit, sondern auch die Bewegungsfreiheit in der Öffentlichkeit für das Entstehen von Literatur ist. Und Patti Smith soll mal in einem Radio-Interview auf die Frage, wie sie sich auf live Auftritte vorbereitet, gesagt haben: »Ich streune für ein paar Stunden durch die Straßen« (»I would roam the streets for a few hours«). Sich frei und alleine in der Öffentlichkeit zu bewegen ist Inspirationsquelle, Erfahrungsraum, Katalysator von Gedanken und Ideen. Und das Umherstreunen Erholung, Müßiggang, Genuss. Wenn in diesem Band Frauen Geschichten über Freiheit erzählen, noch dazu in einem Medium, das lange als männerdominiert galt, tun sie das trotz Care-Arbeit, trotz Street Harrassment, trotz gesellschaftlicher Konventionen. Sie wissen, wovon sie erzählen.

Solange ich kann, solange ich den Luxus freier Zeit genieße, solange mich keine familiären Pflichten abhalten, solange mein Körper es zulässt, werde ich also in den Straßen herumstreifen, ohne irgendein Ziel außer dem Ort, an dem ich zufällig lande. Ich treibe mich herum. Ich pinkele auf Parkplätze. Ich gebe dem Namen Bordsteinschwalbe eine neue Bedeutung. Ich will breitbeinig in der Mitte einer Bank sitzen, mit offenem Mund Kaugummi kauen, sichtbar keinen BH tragen – und ich will nichts hören. Keine Sprüche, keine Blicke. Mehr noch, ich will per Anhalter fahren, ich will betrunken durch nachtleere Straßen laufen, ich will nackt am FKK-Strand liegen. Ich will alleine in einer Bar sitzen und mit fremden Leuten ins Gespräch kommen, ohne misstrauisch zu sein. Ich will mehr als ein Zimmer für mich allein, ich will die Straße. Und ab und zu, wenn es mich überkommt und ich raus gehe, alleine und ohne Ziel, gehört sie mir.

Jule Hoffmann

I put my shoes on, run down the stairs, and let the door lock behind me. I start walking without a thought, with no intentions, without a goal. Everything that was important a moment ago, is left behind in the apartment. A light feeling overcomes me, like going outside without a jacket on for the first time after a long winter. I can now do whatever I feel like doing. Buy a coffee, people and dog watching, observe the facades of houses that I have passed carelessly a thousand times before, or just simply walk. Feeling the rhythm of the steps, the warmth that arises in my body.
I'm anonymous on busy streets. I can be everything and no one. The walk is a free space, an escape, a breakout from all functional contexts. Purposefully, I stroll slowly past the shops, the hectic traffic, people with appointments and goals. While walking, I become an outsider, a dropout. My aimless wandering around is a refusal to work, a short vacation, a demonstration against the efficiency that is dictated by capitalism.
This type of walk is completely different from the casual chatty stroll for two, which was now the only remaining and quickly exhausted social setting in the pandemic. It also has nothing to do with the banal, conservative Sunday stroll in nature. I walk alone. Walking alone can signify radical freedom. You can act on any of your impulses. You can apply yourself as a benchmark just by paying attention to your own needs. You don't have to be considerate, nor reluctant, nor careful, nor quiet, nor empathetic, nor polite, nor reassuring, nor helpful, nor evasive. I call it the radical walk.
The ability to be alone in public as a woman is a freedom that needs to be defended. Against opinions, against stares, against one's own fear. In her book »Wanderlust«, the American writer Rebecca Solnit describes how the possibility of sexual violence is implicitly lurking in remarks, suggestive glances and intimidation, and how the freedom of movement in public spaces is limited and curtailed for women. Solnit also describes that in 19th century Europe, women who walked the streets without clearly identifiable intentions were suspected of prostitution. Being outdoors alone was practically equated with sexual availability. The 19th century has long passed, but part of it still seems to remain, or why do I sometimes feel uncomfortable when I am lying alone by the lake. The streets have always belonged to men, and women

were sent to private rooms where domestic chores were waiting for them. It all sounds like the 19th century, but during the Corona crisis, women, in particular, went back to working part-time in order to take care of the children at home. Following the motto: this is how it has always been done.

The access to public spaces, self-determined participation in public life, being visible and independent, and not having to talk to anyone in the process (or even being able to talk to everyone without being afraid of unintentionally signaling yourself off as prey) should be a fundamental freedom for everyone. In her famous essay, »A room of one's own«, Virginia Woolf wrote about how important it was to have both economic independence and the freedom of movement in public spaces to create literature. And during a radio interview, when Patti Smith was asked how she prepared for live performances, she was quoted as saying »I would roam the streets for a few hours«. Moving freely and alone in public is a source of inspiration, a space for experiences, a catalyst for thoughts and ideas. And the recreational wandering about, idleness, indulgence. When women tell stories about freedom in this volume, especially within a medium that has long been considered to be male-dominated, they do so despite care work, despite street harassment, despite social conventions. They know what they're talking about.

So for as long as I can, for as long as I am able to enjoy the luxury of free time, for as long as family responsibilities do not keep me from it, for as long as my body allows, I'll roam the streets without a predetermined destination except for wherever I happen to end up. I hang around. I pee in parking lots. I'm giving the name streetwalker a new meaning. I want to sit in the middle of a bench with my legs spread apart, chew gum with my mouth open, visibly not wear a bra – and I don't want to hear anything. No comments, no stares. I want even more than that, I want to hitchhike, I want to drunkenly walk through empty streets at night, I want to lie naked on a nudist beach. I want to sit alone in a bar and talk to strangers without being wary. I want more than a room of my own I want the street. And every now and then, when I feel like going out alone without a predetermined destination, it belongs to me.

Jule Hoffmann

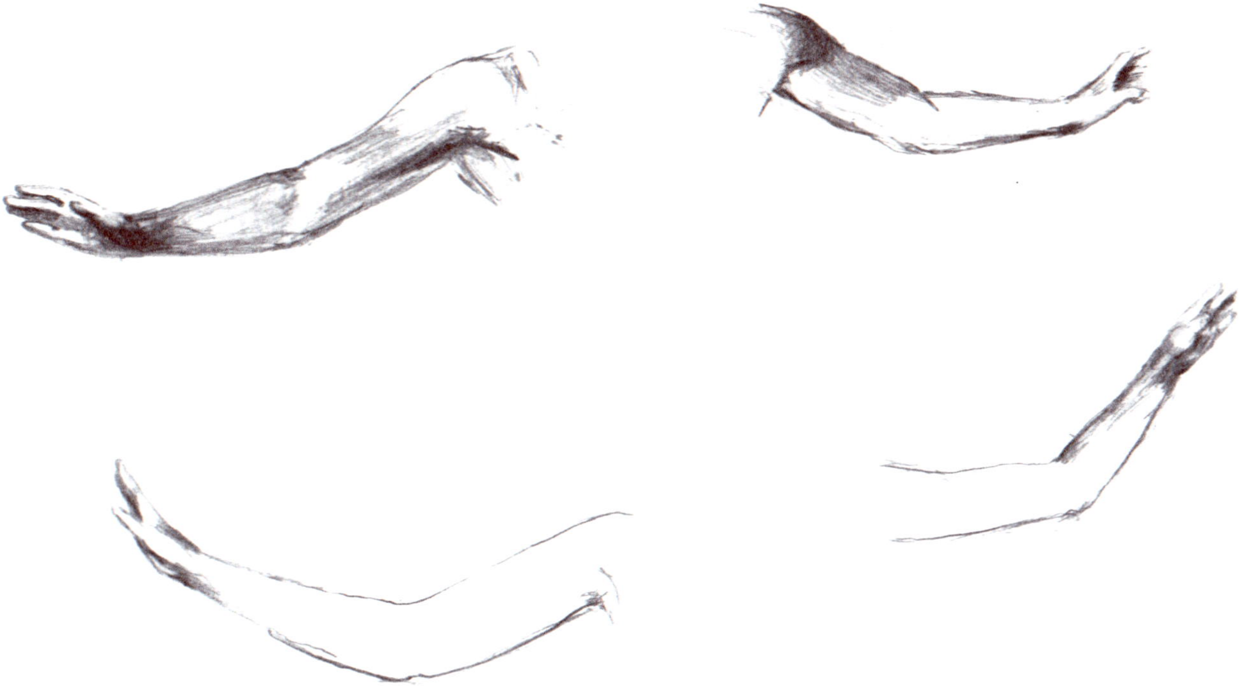

FREIHEIT –
...oder nur ein Gefühl

FREEDOM – again, just a feeling

Tame to the touch / muzzled • A rock in turbulent waters / with the wind in my hair • Beschämt, weil mich jemand dabei ertappt, als ich in den Spiegel schaue • because we are all people / who have to be leaving soon

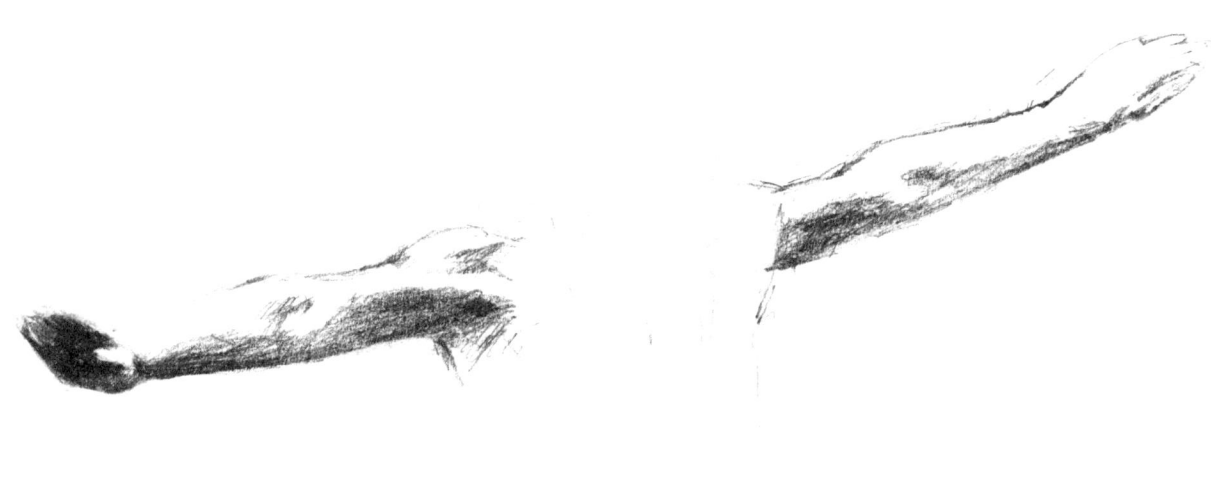

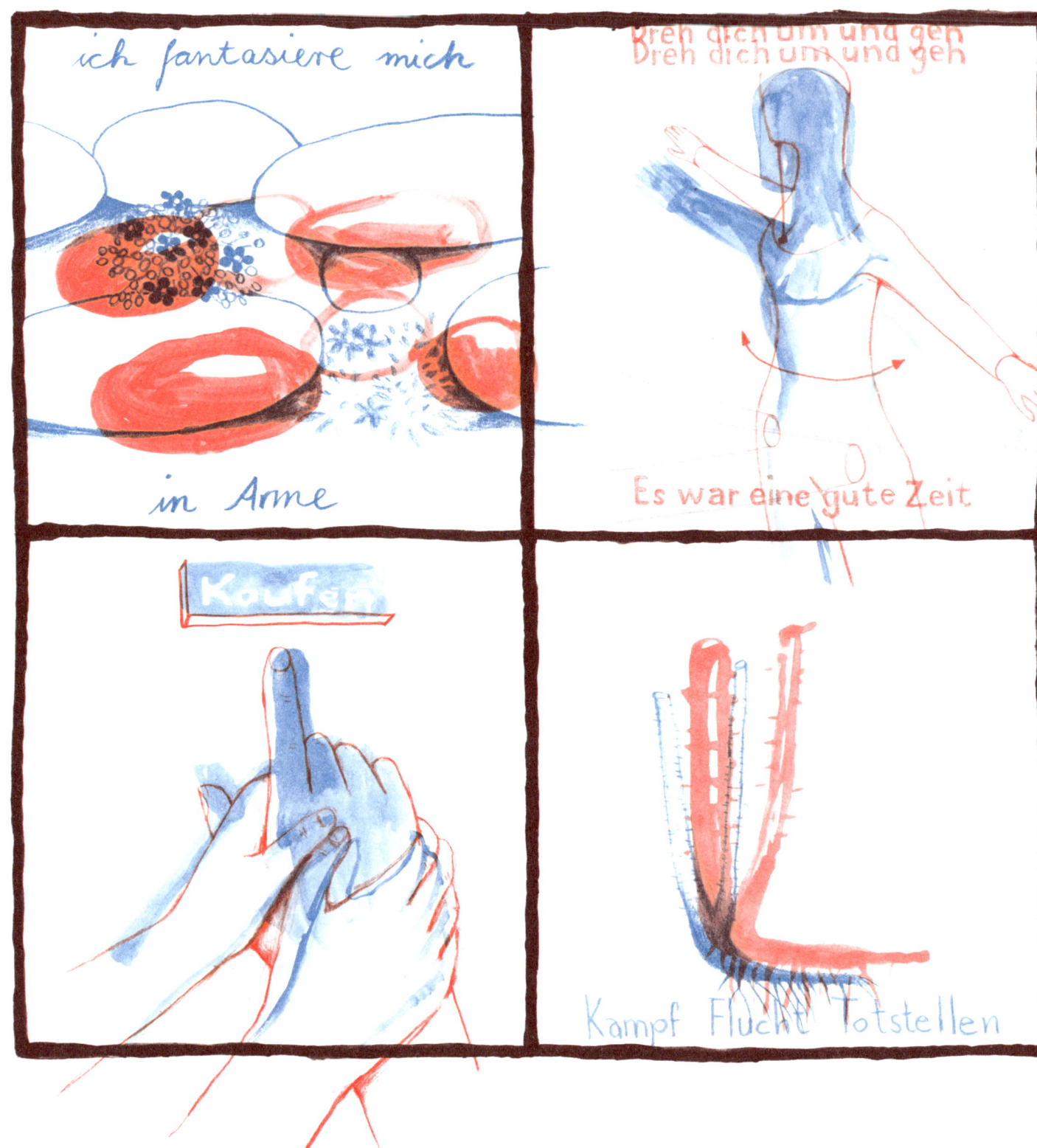

I fantasize about being in arms • Turn around and go / It was a good time • Buy • Fight flight feigning death

from YES to YES-AND-NO • Kill your darlings / yes? • because each person is simultaneously every person they have not become.

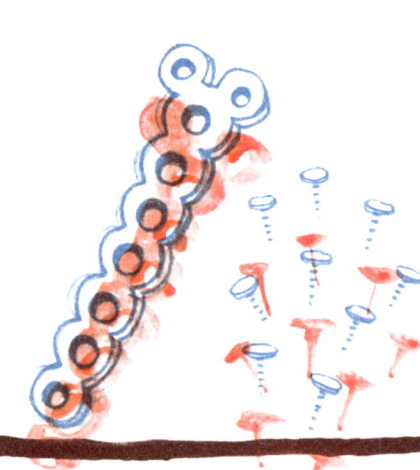

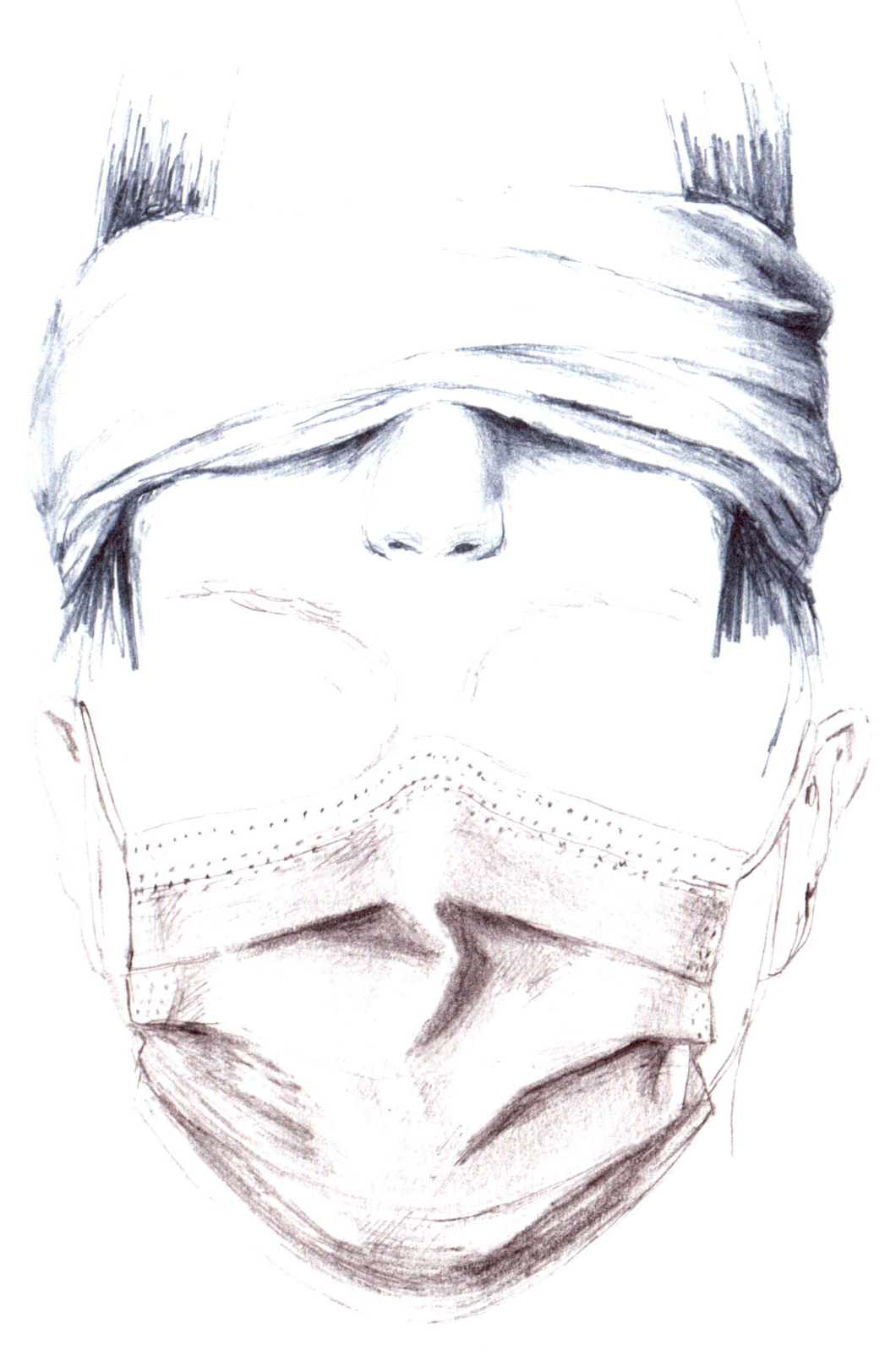

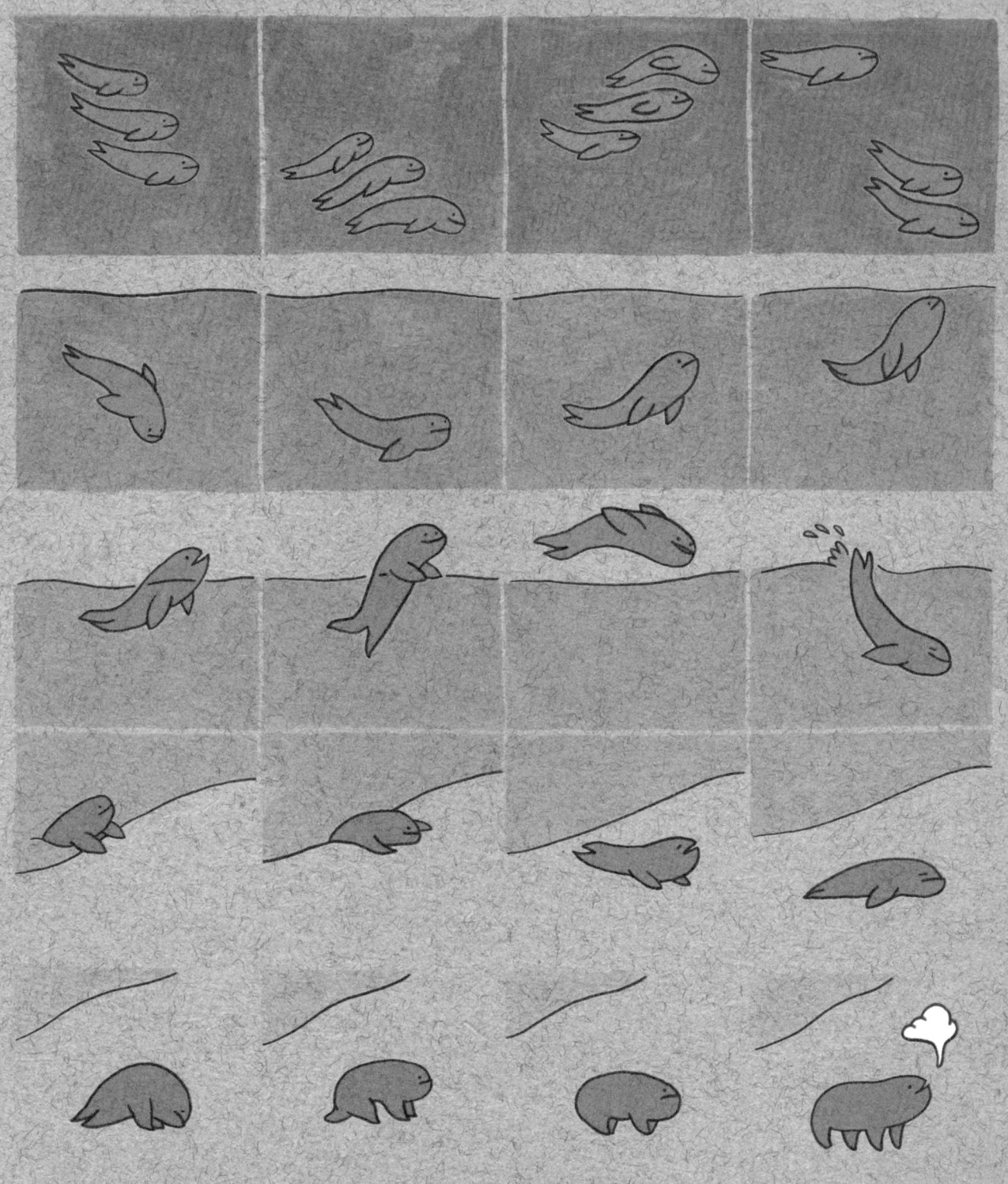

EH NICHTS PASSIERT

ALS ICH VIER WAR, ZOG MEINE FAMILIE IN DIE STRASSE AM DÜRREN AST AM RANDE DES SIEBENTISCHWALDES. NAMEN, WIE FÜR EIN KIND AUSGEDACHT. SIEBEN TISCHE DECKTE ICH DORT MIT GESAMMELTEN KASTANIEN FÜR DIE SIEBEN ZWERGE.

VON STEPHANIE WUNDERLICH

Nothing happened anyway / When I was four, my family moved to a street called *On the dry branch* at the edge of the *Seven Table Forest*. Names, as if made for children. That's were I set seven tables with chestnuts that I collected for the seven dwarfs.

IM WALD GAB ES VIELE RUNDE GRUBEN. DAS WAREN BOMBENTRICHTER AUS DEM KRIEG, DENN FRÜHER STAND IN DER NÄHE EINE RÜSTUNGSFABRIK. EINMAL FANDEN WIR DEN EINGANG ZU EINEM UNTERIRDISCHEN BUNKER DER MESSERSCHMITT FABRIK. NATÜRLICH WAR ES VERBOTEN DORT HINEINZUGEHEN. WIR SPIELTEN HEIMLICH GESPENSTERJÄGER. LEIDER WURDE DER BUNKER WENIG SPÄTER, NOCH BEVOR WIR EIN GESPENST FANGEN KONNTEN, ZUGESCHÜTTET.

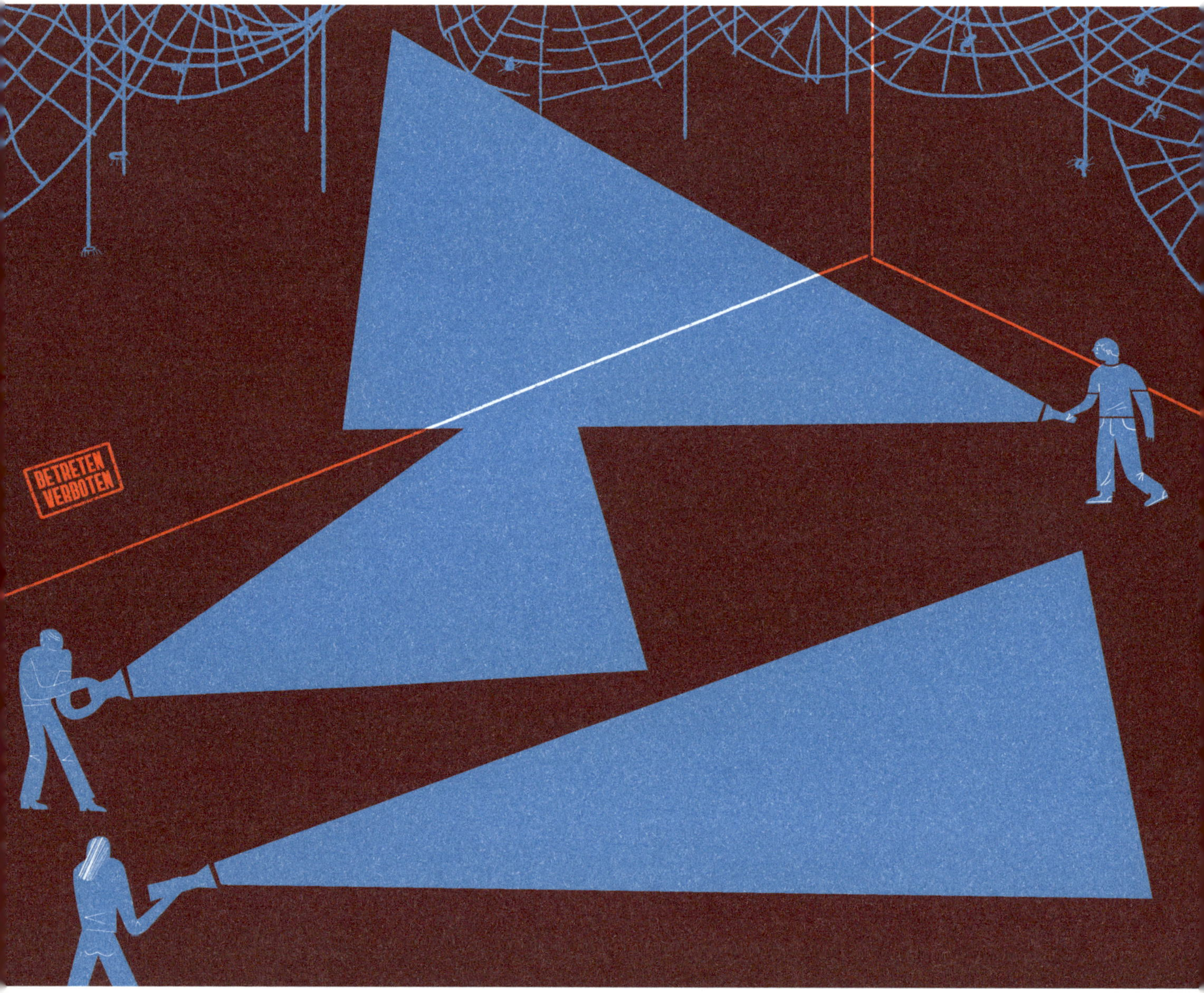

There were many round pits in the forest. They were bomb craters from the war because there used to be an armament factory nearby. We once found the entrance to an underground bunker of the Messerschmitt factory. Of course, entering wasn't allowed. We secretly played ghost hunters. Unfortunately, shortly after we'd found it and before we were able to catch a ghost, the bunker had been filled up with soil. / Do Not Enter

IN DEN WALDWEGEN STANDEN MANCHMAL MÄNNER, UNS ZUGEWANDT, MIT HERUNTERGELASSENEN HOSEN. WIR RASTEN MIT GELÄCHTER VORBEI.

BEI UNSEREN MÜTTERN KLINGELTEN WIR, WENN ETWAS ARG BLUTETE.

ABENDS RIEFEN DIE ELTERN IHRE KINDER ZUM ESSEN.

IN DEN REIHENAUSGÄRTEN UNTER DEM BLICK DER MÜTTER SPIELTEN WIR KAUM. IM WALD, AUF DEN WIESEN DAVOR, DEM ÜBUNGSPLATZ DES SCHÄFERHUNDVEREINS, AM BACHLAUF UND IN DER VERLASSENEN HOLZHÜTTE WAREN WIR UNGESTÖRT UND ERLEBTEN VIELE ABENTEUER.

Sometimes there'd be men standing on the paths in the forest, facing us, with their pants down. We raced past them with laughter. We rang the bells of our mothers when something was badly bleeding. In the evenings, parents called their children home to eat. We hardly played in the yards of the townhouses, under our mothers' watchful eyes. In the forest, on the meadows along the edge, by the shepherd dog club practice area, by the stream, and in the abandoned wooden hut is where we had many adventures and played uninterrupted.

ALS TEENIE LANGWEILTE ICH MICH IM REIHENHAUSGARTEN. DIE BESTE FREUNDIN WAR WEGGEZOGEN. DIE JUNGS UND ICH – WIR GINGEN SCHÜCHTERN UND SPERRIG MITEINANDER UM, DIE INNIGE VERTRAUTHEIT DER KINDERTAGE WAR VERFLOGEN.

ICH WAR OFT TRAURIG UND VERMISSTE DIESE UNBESCHWERTHEIT.

As a teen, the townhouse neighborhood was boring. My best friend had moved away. The boys and I – we were shy and awkward with each other. The intimate familiarity of our childhood days had passed. I was often sad and missed that lightheartedness.

For weeks, I'd ride my bike aimlessly through the forest every afternoon and felt freer.

Only once I reached the reservoir, among the many other people, did I have the courage to stop and look back.

After that experience, I could no longer ride in the forest alone. / Restricted area, prohibited area, stop, no-go, halt, green hell

WENN ICH MEINE FREUNDE AM SEE TREFFEN WOLLTE, NAHM ICH UMWEGE ÜBER DAS STADTGEBIET IN KAUF, UM NUR DIE LETZTEN 600 M DURCH DEN WALD ZU FAHREN.

KAM MIR EIN MANN ENTGEGEN, POCHTE MEIN HERZ UND ICH MUSSTE MICH ZWANGHAFT UMDREHEN. NUR UM SICHERZUGEHEN, DASS ER AUCH WIRKLICH NICHT DIE RICHTUNG WECHSELTE.

ICH TRAUTE MICH NICHT, MEINEN SCHÜCHTERNEN FREUND MARC, DER NEBEN MIR WOHNTE, ZU FRAGEN, OB WIR DEN WEG NICHT ZUSAMMEN FAHREN KÖNNTEN. UNGLAUBLICH ERLEICHTERT WÄRE ICH GEWESEN, EINE BEGLEITUNG ZU HABEN, ABER ES WAR MIR PEINLICH, MEINE ANGST ZUZUGEBEN. DENN ES WAR JA EH NICHTS PASSIERT AUF DEM WEG AM FLUSS.

When I wanted to meet up with my friends at the lake, I'd take detours through the city area so that I would only need to ride the last 600 m through the forest. If a man passed me while riding in the opposite direction, my heart would pound and I'd obsessively look back just to make sure that he really hadn't turned around. I didn't have the courage to ask my shy friend Marc, who lived next door to me, to ride along the way with me. I would have been incredibly relieved to have someone ride with me, but I was embarrassed to admit to my fear. Because nothing had happened on the way to the river, anyway.

Dile Aadam

Das Herz des Menschen / the heart of man

 Das Herz

 des Menschen

 will aus den Augen

 der ganzen Welt lesen.

Dile aadam mesha chasme hama dunya ra bekhaanad.
The heart of man wants to see through all the eyes of the world.

Das Herz des Menschen will die Geheimnisse aller Herzen kennen.

Dile aadam mesha raaze hama del ha ra bedaanad.
The heart of man wants to know the secrets of all hearts.

Das Herz   des Menschen

will an das   Leben glauben.

Dile Aadam mesha baawar bekonad zindagi ra.
The heart of man wants to believe in life.

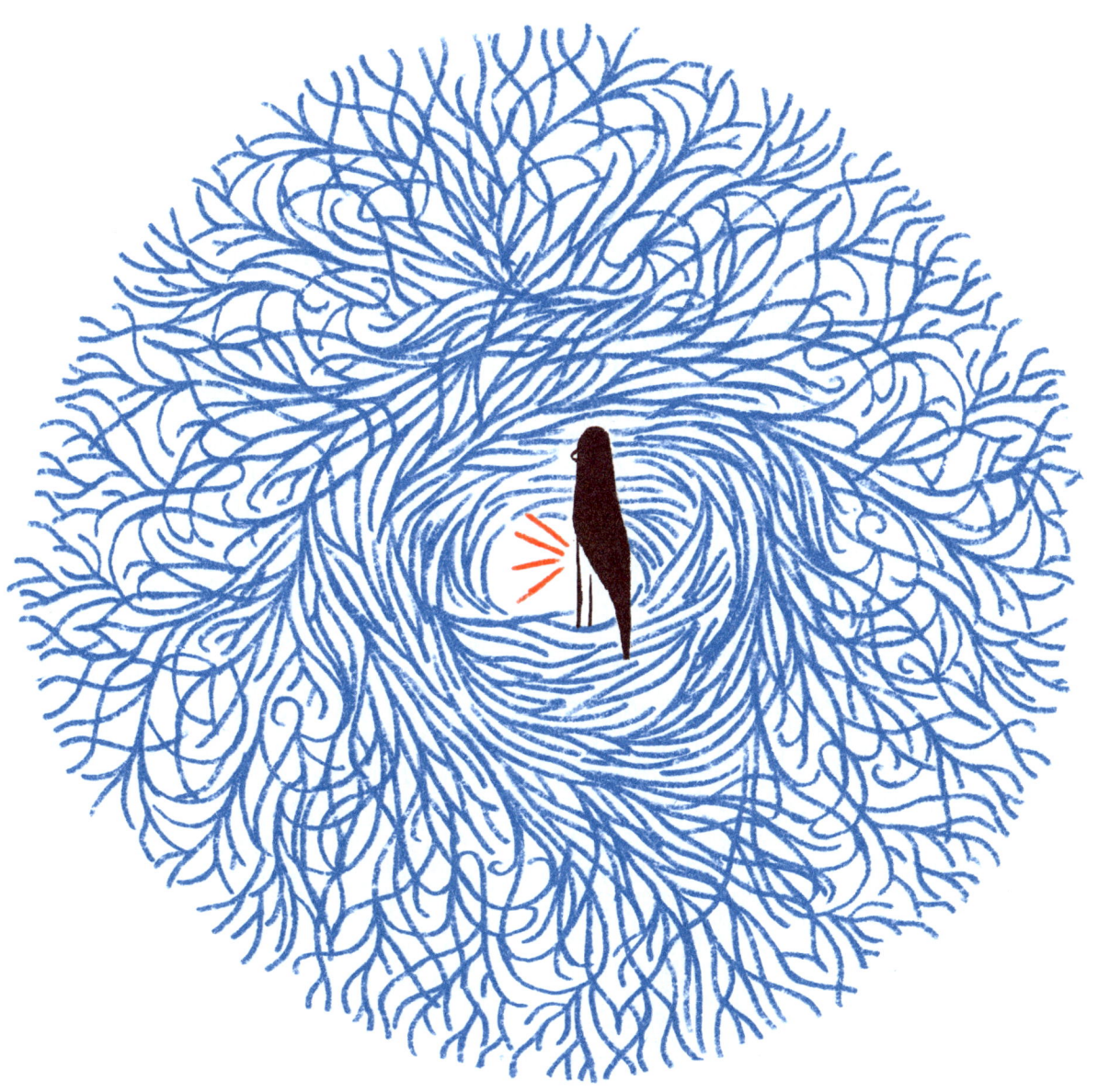

Das Herz des Menschen will frei von allen Sorgen sein.

Dile aadam mesha as chod hama chramhaa ra beranad.

The heart of man wants to be free from all sorrows.

Wie eitel

sind die

Begierden

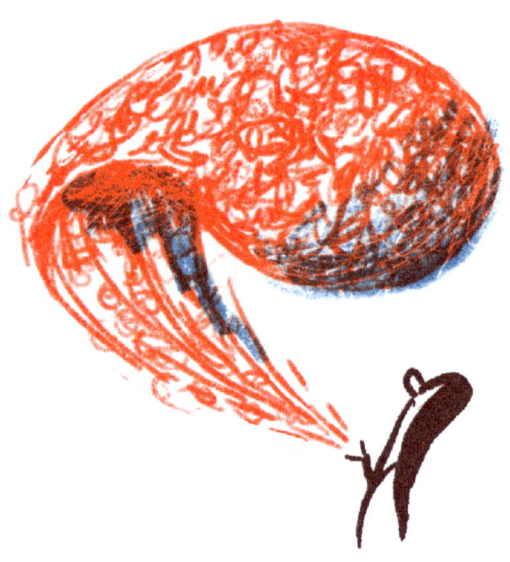
des Herzens?

Dile aadam cheqarda khaaheshe bejaa mekonad?
How vain are the desires of the heart?

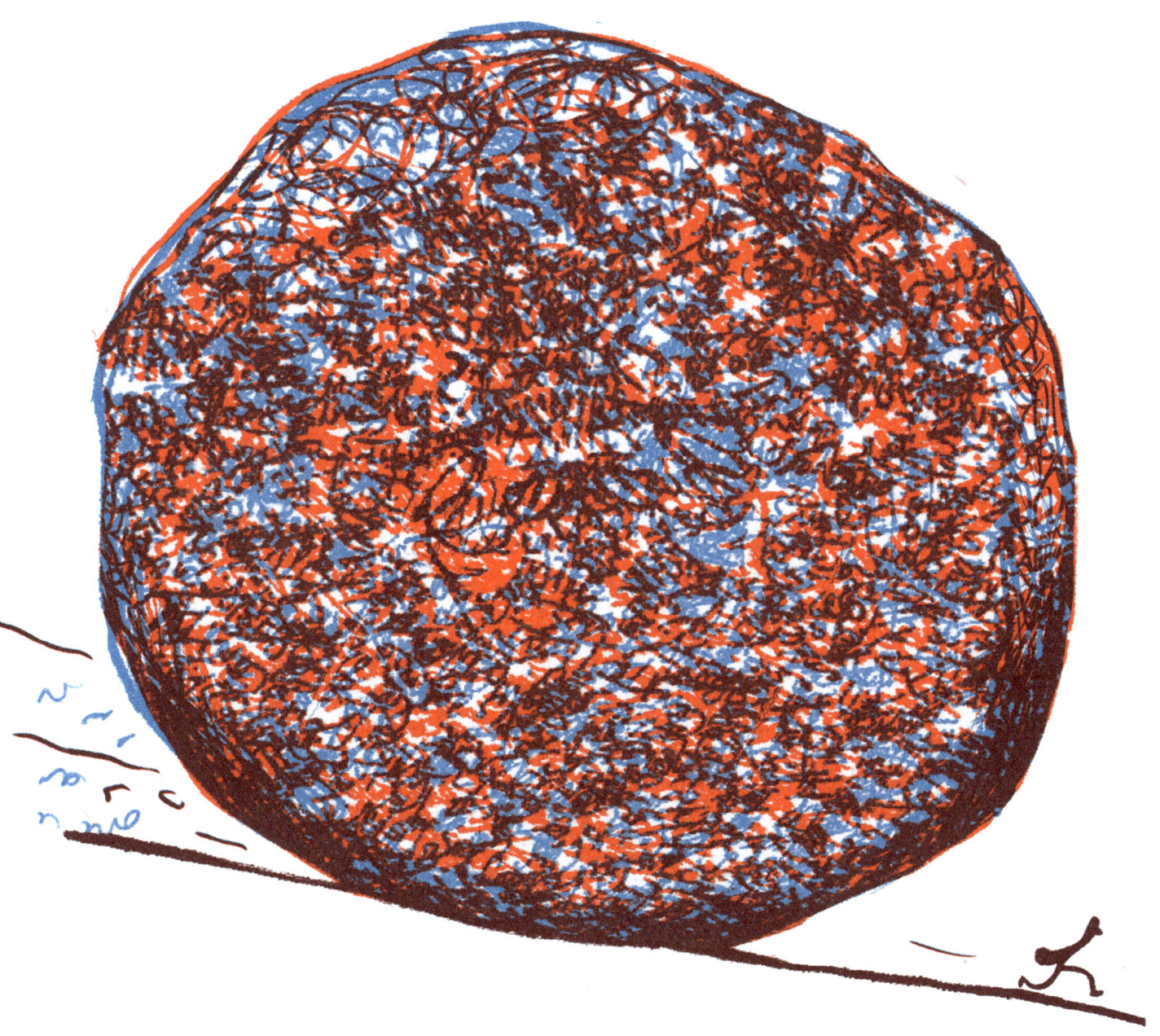

Bei Gott, das Herz beschämt den Menschen.

Dile aadam ba khoda aadama ruswaa mekonad.
By God, the heart can disgrace man with its desires.

Listen to the song

Dile Aadam ist ein Gedicht des afghanischen Poeten Sakhi Rahi (1915-2009).

Der Musiker Waheed Qasemi hat in den 90er Jahren zu dem Gedicht ein Lied komponiert, das von der Sängerin Parasto interpretiert wurde.
Beide sind bekannte afghanische Musiker*innen und Dile Aadam war ihr letztes in Afghanistan veröffentlichtes Lied. Parasto lebt in Hannover, Deutschland. Waheed Quasemi in Toronto, Kanada.

Dile Aadam is a poem written by the Afghan poet Sakhi Rahi (1915-2009).

The musician Waheed Qasemi composed a song to the poem in the 90s, which was interpreted by the singer Parasto.
Both are well-known Afghan musicians and Dile Aadam was their last song published in Afghanistan. Parasto lives in Hannover, Germany. Waheed Quasemi lives in Toronto, Canada.

Masks are mandatory here, put it on IMMEDIATELY. / Woah, it's cold. I'd rather be inside reading a good book. / Ah good, there's a trash can for the poop bag. / HEY, SUCK IN YOUR BELLY!

Die Verantwortung beginnt im Traum!
In dreams begin responsibilities

Träume sind dafür da, Dinge zu tun, die man nicht in der Realität tun kann.
Dreams make it possible to do things you can't do in reality.

Du hast echt Luxus-Probleme!
You have luxury problems!

Du kannst nicht einfach alles hinschmeißen!
You can't just throw it all away!

Du musst etwas ändern!
You have to change something!

Brich aus!
Break out!

Kämpf dich frei!
Fight your way free!

Denk auch mal an Dich!
Think of yourself for a change too!

Emanzipier Dich!
Emancipate yourself!

Du bist nicht das Maß aller Dinge!
You are not the center of the universe!

Tu dies, tu das!
Do this, do that!

Mach doch 'ne Therapie!
Get some therapy!

Du kannst nicht nur an dich denken!
You can't just think about yourself!

Komm in die Gänge!
Get with the program!

Larissa Bertonasco

Dance!

dedicated to Ahmad Joudeh, Dancer from Damaskus and Sama Abdulhadi, Techno DJ from Ramallah

sometimes the only escape from my pain

is to shake it out of me

and those imposed by the world

I long for connection

ich sehne mich nach Verbindung

and to be seen for who I am

und als die gesehen zu werden, die ich bin

there are times and places where we resist
and become freedom fighters only by chance

es gibt Zeiten und Orte, wo wir Widerstand leisten und nur durch Zufall zu Freiheitskämpfer*innen werden

Aufrauschen
Almuth Ertl

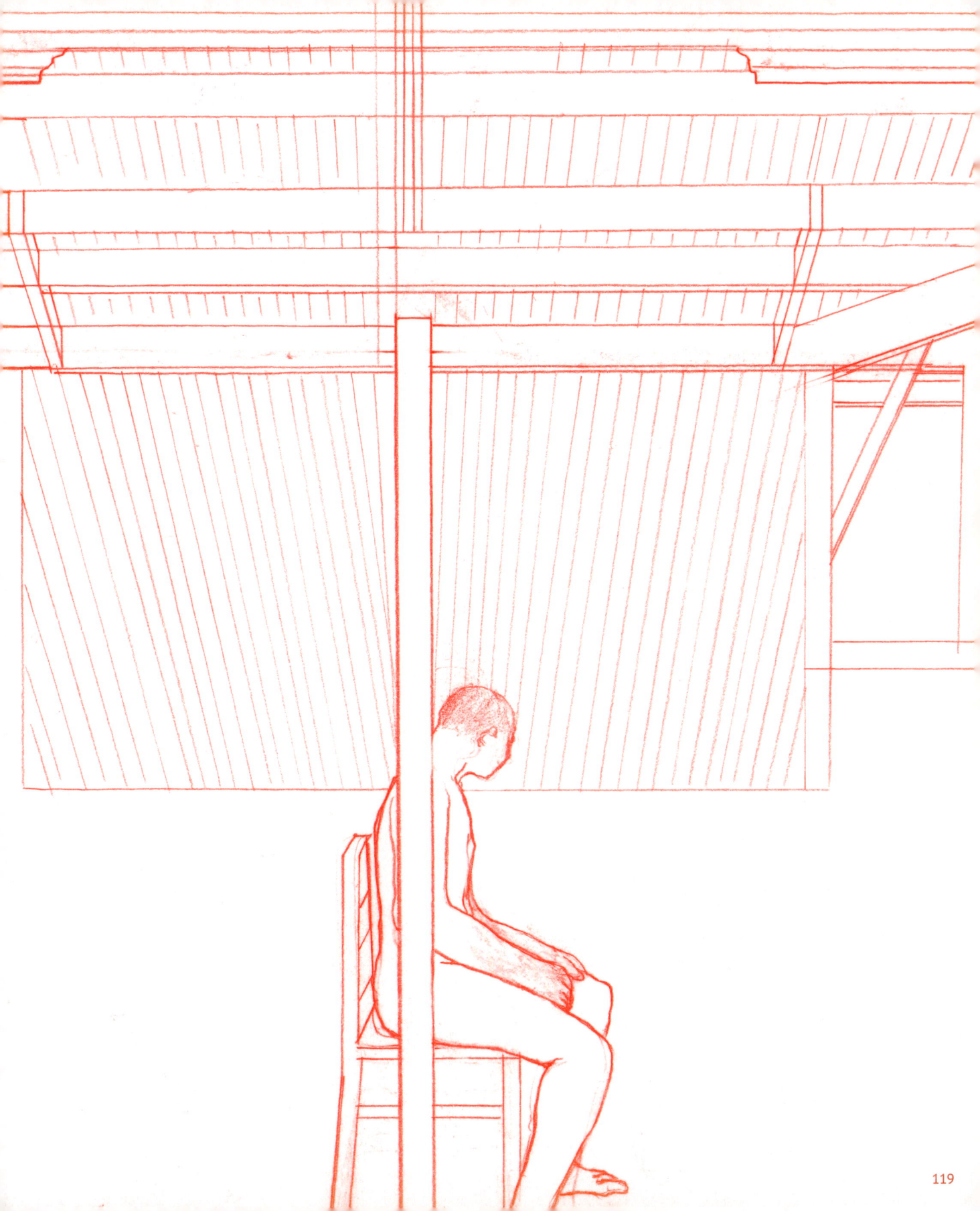

Absolute Freiheit bedeutet absolute Verantwortung.

Gehorsam schützt die Freiheit.

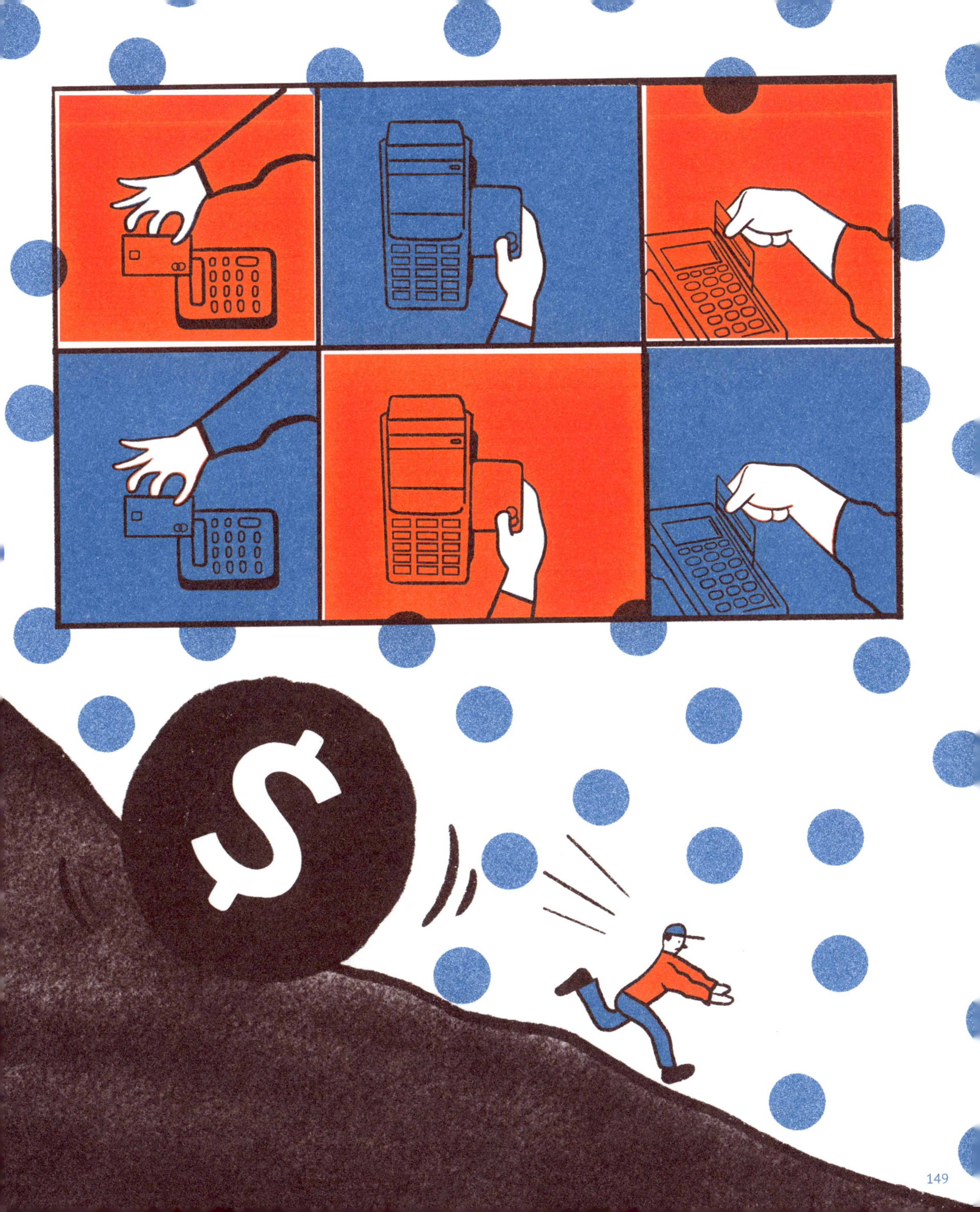

DOES ABSOLUTE FREEDOM ACTUALLY EXIST ?

Gibt es die absolute Freiheit tatsächlich?

I MUST HAVE THE COURAGE TO BREAK AWAY FROM LUSTFULNESS AND TO NOT THINK MUCH ABOUT WHAT OTHER PEOPLE THINK OF ME.

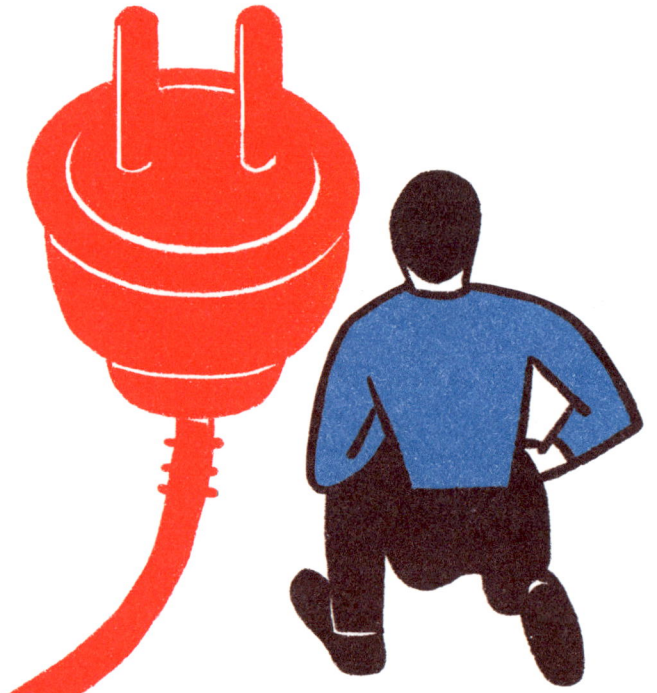

THEN YOU WILL KNOW THE TRUTH,
AND THE TRUTH WILL SET YOU FREE.

THANKS TO JOSE CAROL & JEFFREY RACHMAT.

Dann wirst du die Wahrheit erkennen, und die Wahrheit wird dich frei machen. Dank an Jose Carol & Jeffrey Rachmat.

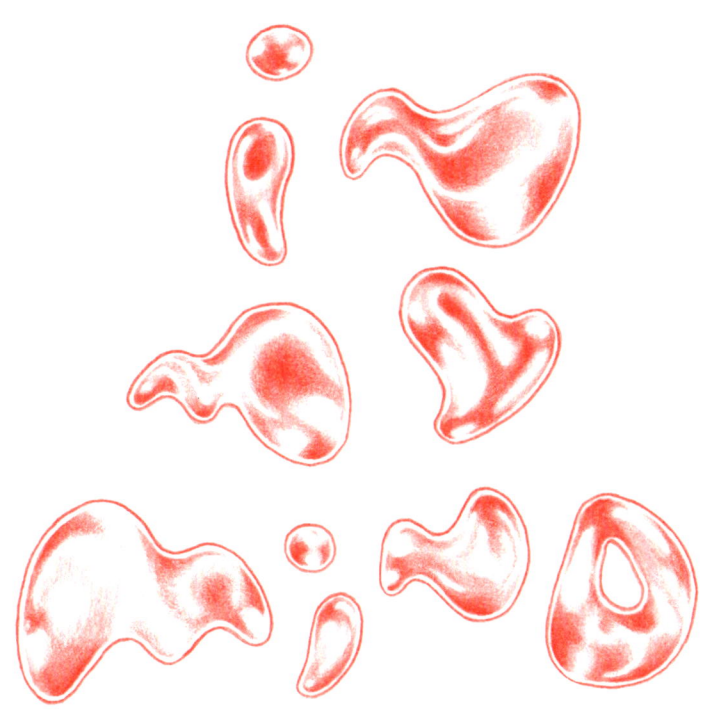

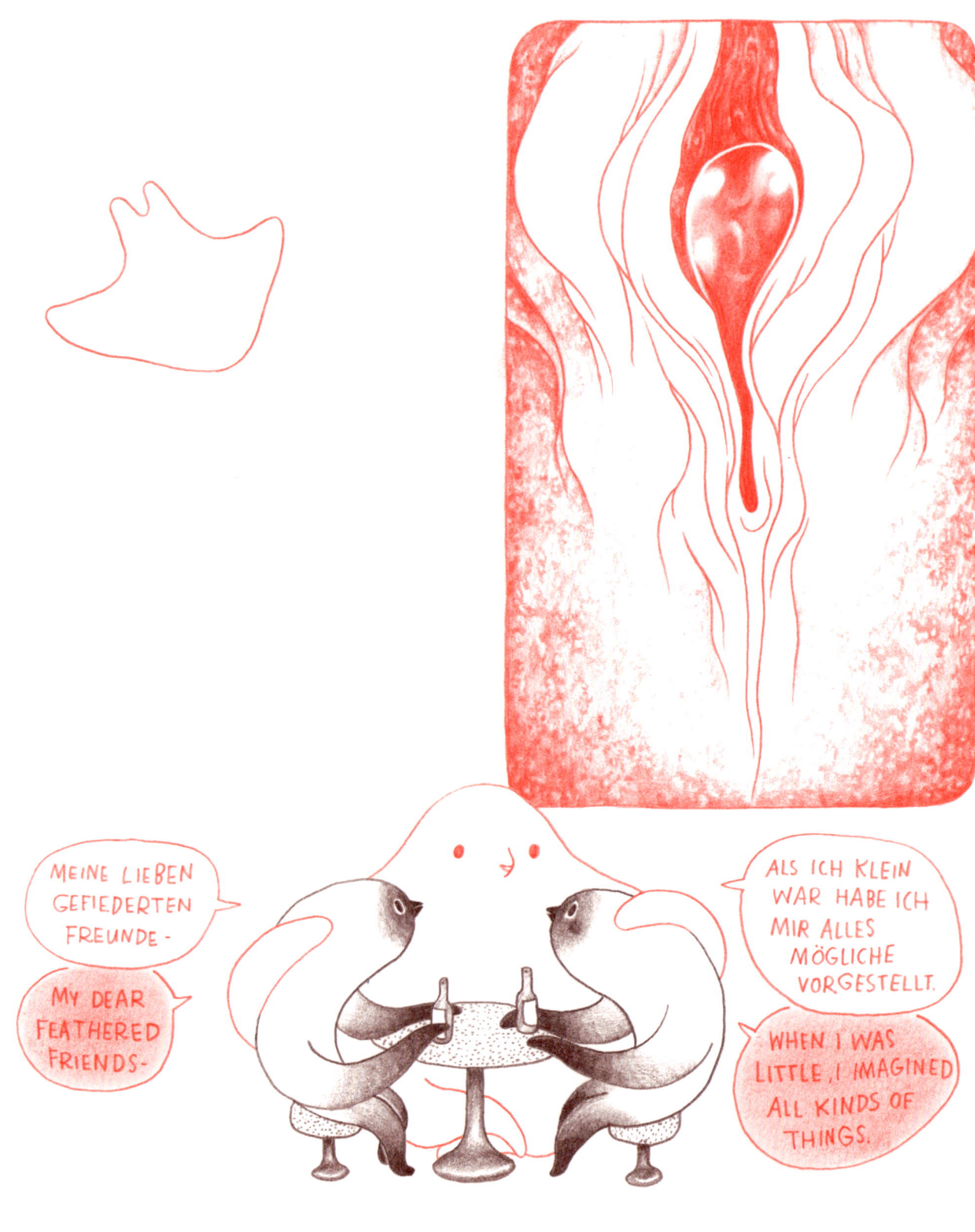

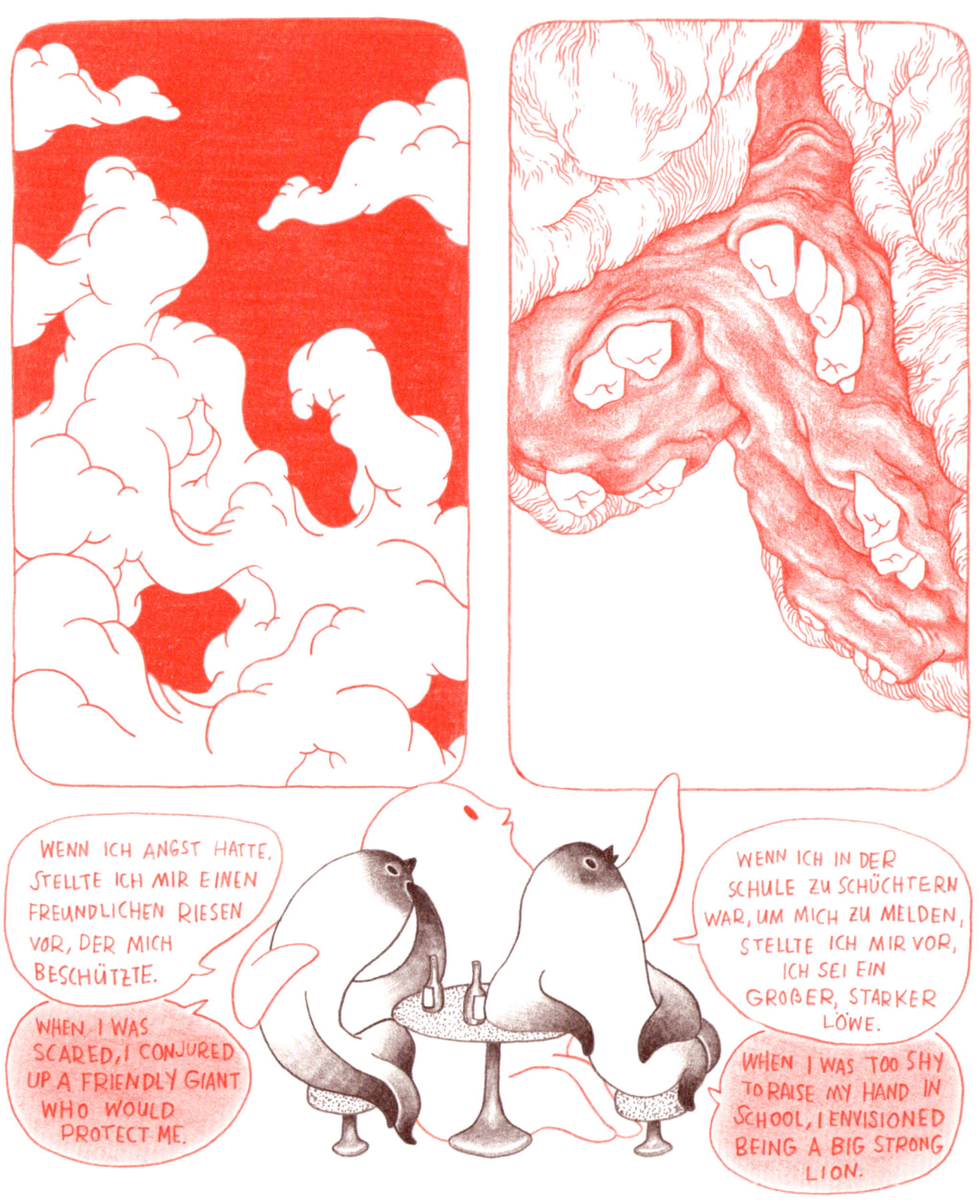

Goose in Luck – Loosely based on Hans in Luck

What's going on here?

Enough is enough, get lost / ha, oh well

You stink • You are way too fat • You are boring • Your neck's too long • Too-oooo fast • Your ears are too big • Tooo weird • You smoke too much • You have too much hair

I've done everything on my to do list. / Great, then you can watch netflix now! / Nope. I think I just made too little notes. / Hahaha

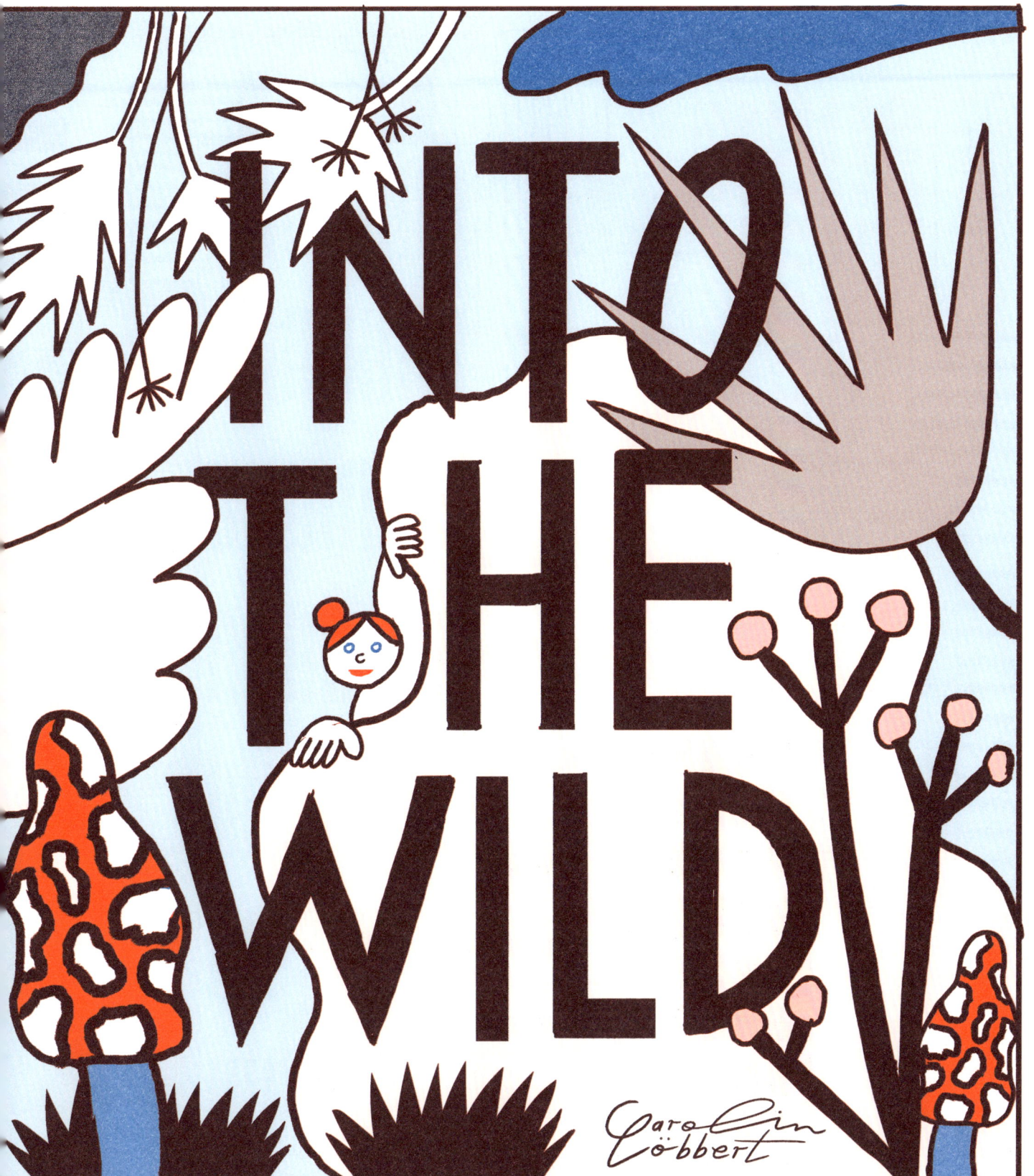

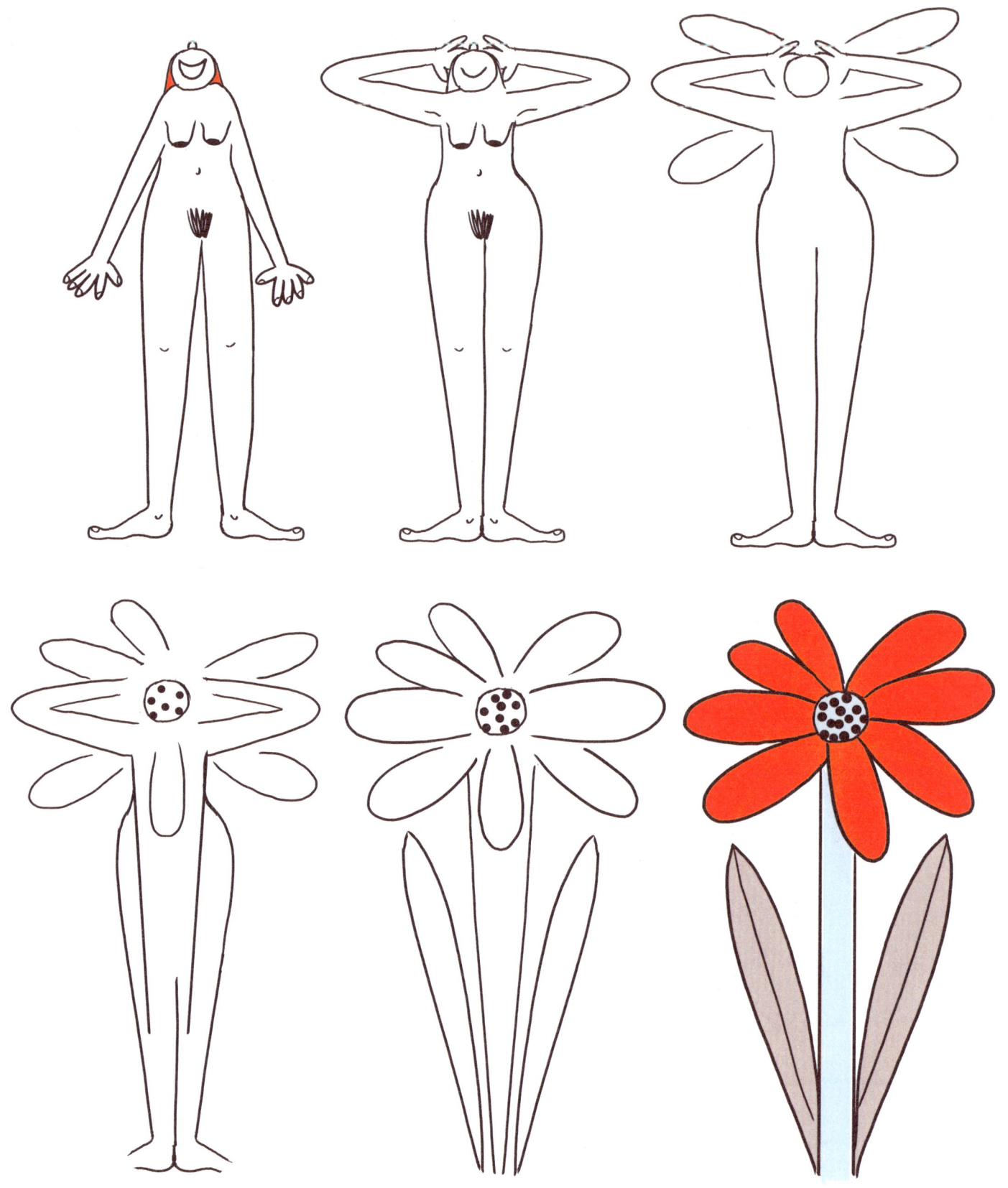

You know, I don't even have a watch. / 'Cause, you know, I'm an artist. / And well, – receiving unemployment benefits.

Anzeigen

3x in Berlin   online www.modern-graphics.de

MODERN GRAPHICS - DER COMICSHOP

Mit Gesa
vorwärts gehen

0176 51610229
info@mitgesa.de
instagram.com/mit_gesa

Access Bars®

Gesa Spreter
von Kreudenstein

AID Akademie für Illustration und Design Berlin

MACH WAS AUS DEINEM TALENT

GESTALTUNG/KOOPERATION: N. RESTLE, 5. Sem. (IDEE)
N. PAGALIES, DOZENTIN (BILD)

krumulus

Buchhandlung, Galerie und Druckwerkstatt für Kinder

Südstern 4
10961 Berlin

krumulus.com

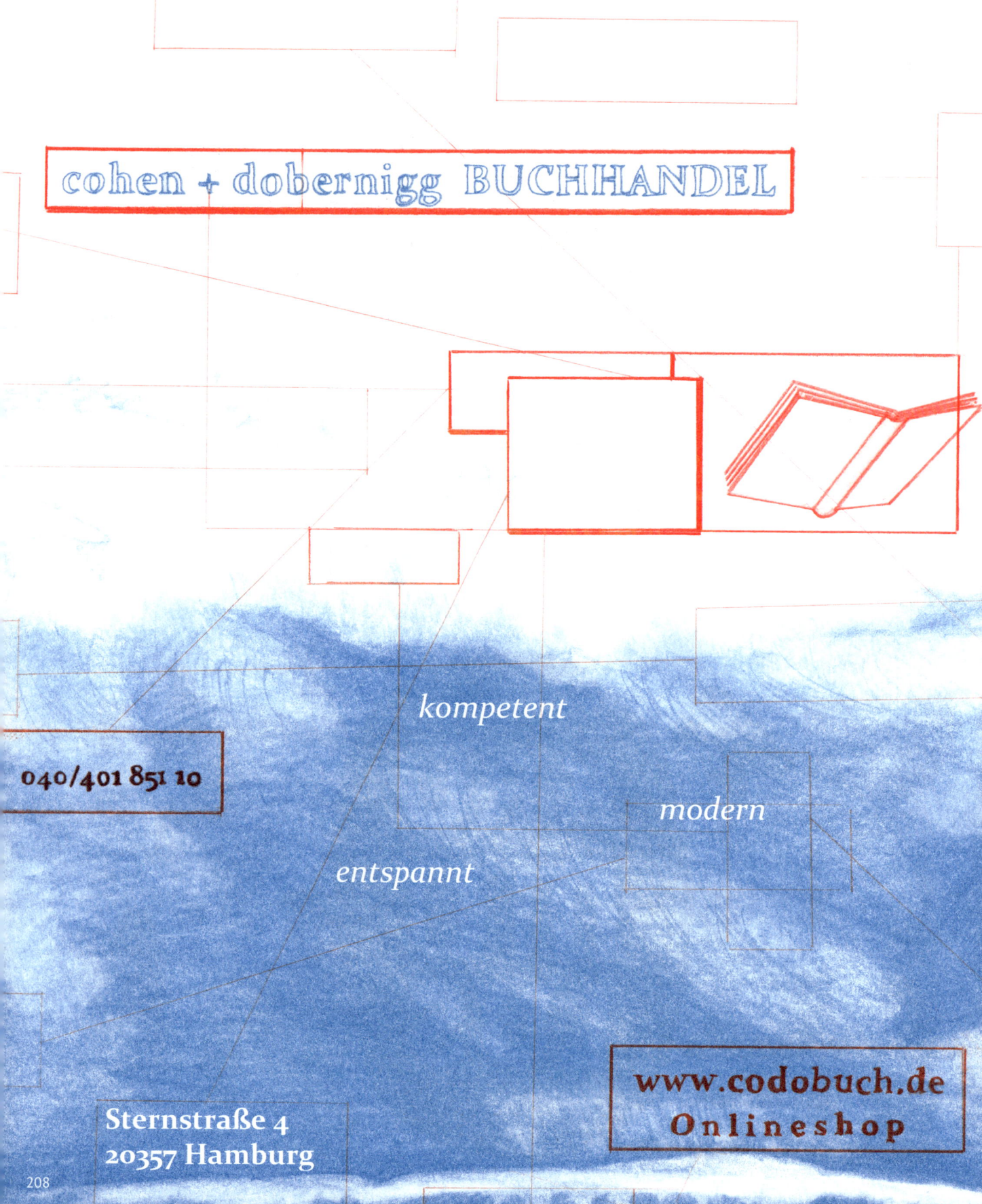

2 AGENTEN
AGENTUR FÜR ILLUSTRATION

MAIL@2AGENTEN.COM
+49 30 4171 467

www.publizieren-im-netz.de

Frei und unabhängig mit deiner Website in WordPress

MARK WEIß WIE'S GEHT!

FRAG' IHN!

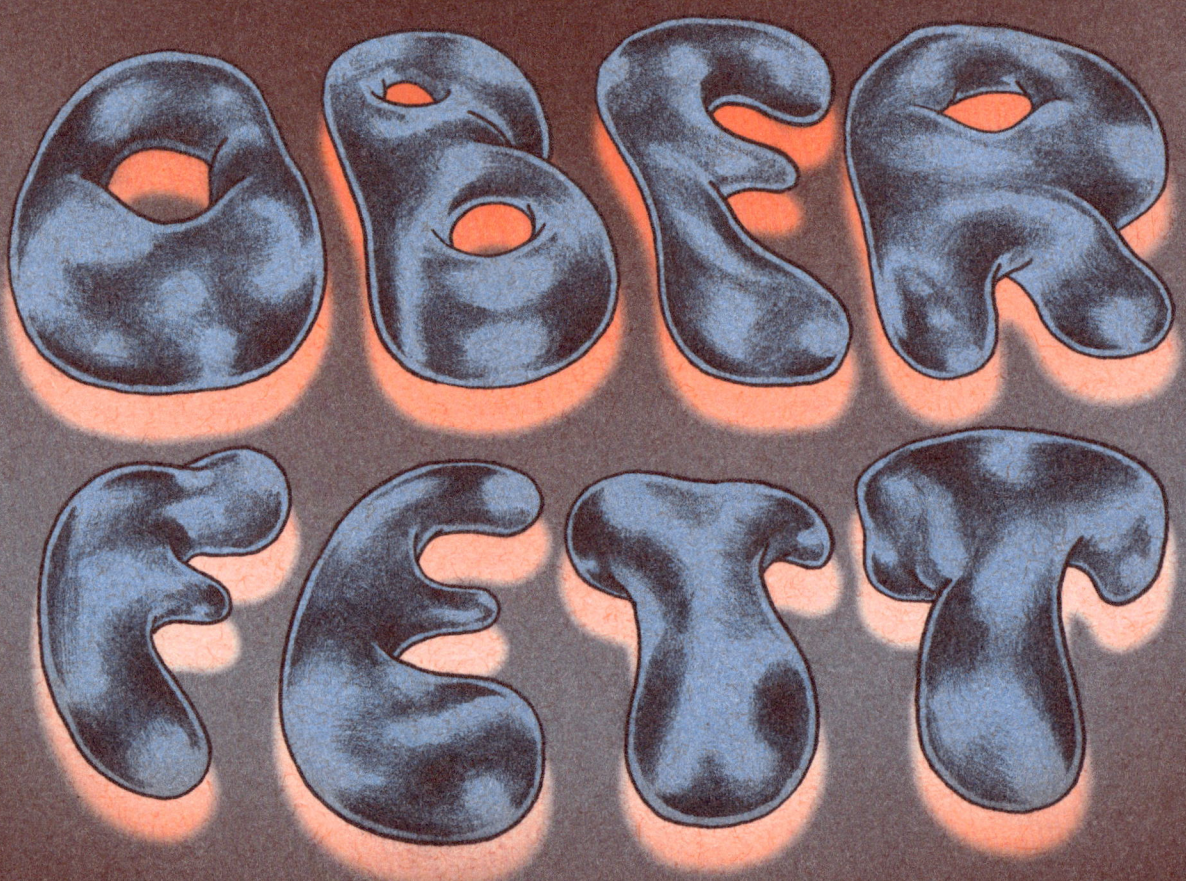

BILDERBUCHMUSEUM
BURG WISSEM
TROISDORF

www.bilderbuchmuseum.de

MaroHefte: Essay & Illustration

mit Originaldruckgraphiken

und beiliegendem Plakat

maroverlag.de

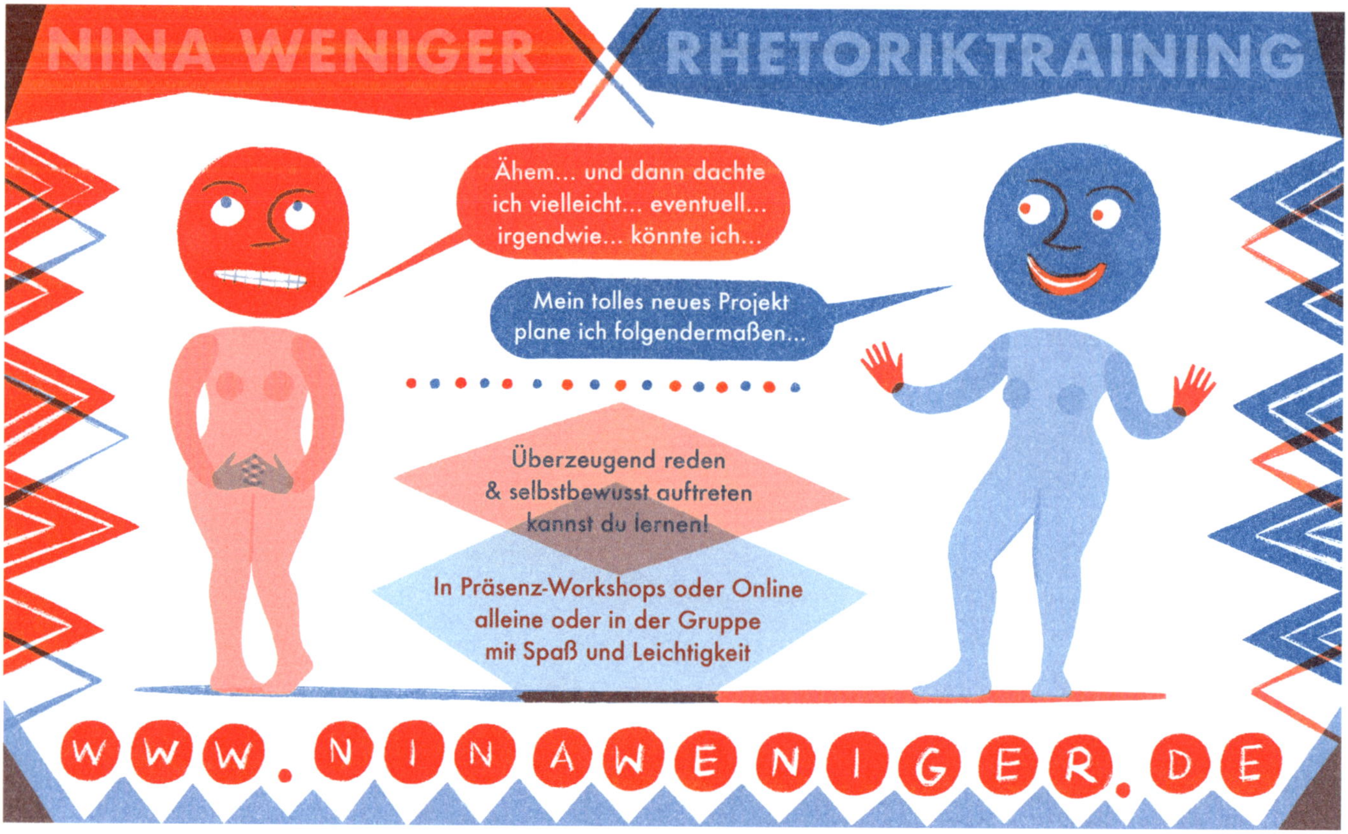
NINA WENIGER
RHETORIKTRAINING
Ähem... und dann dachte ich vielleicht... eventuell... irgendwie... könnte ich...
Mein tolles neues Projekt plane ich folgendermaßen...
Überzeugend reden & selbstbewusst auftreten kannst du lernen!
In Präsenz-Workshops oder Online alleine oder in der Gruppe mit Spaß und Leichtigkeit
WWW.NINAWENIGER.DE

Classic Cycles Hamburg
Rennräder
Klappräder
Hollandräder
Neuer Kamp 30 · 20357 Hamburg

LOGBUCH

L

BÜCHER IM DSM
BREMERHAFEN

BÜCHER IN WALLE
BREMEN

LOGBUCHLADEN.DE

Mit einer Knarre fühlt man sich wie Gott, weißte? / Barf.

Zeichnerinnen

Doris Freigofas wuchs hinter einer Mauer auf, die fiel, als Doris 6 Jahre alt war – zu Doris' großer Unfreude, denn nun konnte sie keine Jungpionierin mehr werden und bekam auch nicht das fesche blaue Halstuch. 32 Jahre später lebt sie in Berlin als freie Illustratorin mit ihrem Partner in wilder Ehe und beide illustrieren gemeinsam als Golden Cosmos für den New Yorker, die New York Times oder die Washington Post. Doris Freigofas grew up behind a wall that fell when Doris was 6 years old – to Doris' great displeasure, because now she could no longer become neither a Young Pioneer nor get the smart blue neckerchief. 32 years later she lives in Berlin as a freelance illustrator with her partner in a wild marriage. As Golden Cosmos they illustrate together for the New Yorker, the New York Times or the Washington Post. **www.golden-cosmos.com**

marialuisa – Zwischen In-die-Lüfte-Schrauben und Freiem Fall marialuisa – Between spiraling into the air and free falling: **www.marialuisa.de**

moki – über seinen Schatten springen, neue Wege erkunden, anders denken – in ihren drei Geschichten für SPRING #18 wachsen mokis Protagonisten auf unterschiedliche Weisen über sich hinaus: in ihrem Freiheitsbestreben überwinden sie rein physische Grenzen und triggern die Evolution, sie wagen sich ins Reich der Fantasie, um mentale Kraft zu schöpfen und sie verlieren sich im Dickicht des eigenen, unausgesprochenen Begehrens, um gesellschaftlich etablierte Strukturen zu hinterfragen. Die Verantwortung, sich von starren Strukturen zu befreien, liegt oft bei uns selbst. Die Frage in einer Gesellschaft ist jedoch, wo endet die des einen und wo beginnt die des anderen? **moki** – Jumping over one's shadow, exploring new paths, thinking differently – in their three stories for SPRING #18, moki's protagonists grow beyond themselves in different ways: in their quest for freedom they overcome purely physical boundaries and trigger evolution, they venture into the realm of fantasy, as they draw in mental strength and lose themselves in a thicket of their own, unspoken desire to question socially established structures. The responsibility to free ourselves from rigid structures often rests within ourselves. The question in a society, however, is where does one end and where does another begin? **mioke.de**

Stephanie Wunderlich hat an der FH Augsburg und der ISIA Urbino Kommunikationsdesign studiert. Sie arbeitet von Hamburg aus als freie Illustratorin für internationale Magazine und Designbüros. Stephanie ist seit 2008 Mitherausgebern des Spring Magazins. Die Idee die Geschichte über ihren beängstigenden Waldausflug mit weitreichenden Folgen zu erzählen, kam ihr im März, als sie als artist in residence in Krems/Österreich viele genüssliche Stunden in den Bergen und Wäldern der Wachau alleine wandern ging. Stephanie Wunderlich studied communication design at the Augsburg University of Applied Sciences and the ISIA Urbino. She works as a freelance illustrator in Hamburg for international magazines and design offices. Stephanie has been a co-editor of Spring Magazine since 2008. The idea to tell the story about her frightening forest excursion with far-reaching consequences came to her in March, when she went hiking alone in the mountains and forests of The Wachau in Krems, Austria while she was staying there as an artist in residence. **www.wunderlich-illustration.de**

Maren Amini hat nach Ihrem Illustrations-Studium (an der HAW Hamburg) noch lange im Freibad gearbeitet bis sie endlich freiberufliche Illustratorin wurde. Sie zeichnet für die freie Wirtschaft und verkauft ihre freien Werke in ihrem Laden-Atelier »Fritzen«, neben der Großen Freiheit. Aber freilich auch online unter: www.Maren-Amini.de/shop After having obtained a degree in illustration (from the HAW Hamburg), Maren Amini continued to work at an outdoor pool for a long time until she finally became a freelance illustrator. She draws for ultimate freedom, but also for the free economy and sells her free works in her shop-atelier »Fritzen«. But feel free to view her works online as well: **www.Maren-Amini.de/shop**

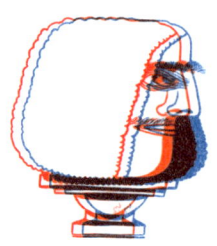

Moshtari Hilal ist bildende Künstlerin und Forscherin und lebt in Hamburg und Berlin. In ihrer zeichnerischen Arbeit untersucht Moshtari die Bildsprache des Subjektiven, des Behaarten und der Linie. So arbeitet die Künstlerin mit der gezeichneten Linie als Mittel und Symbol, welche sich auf den schwarzhaarigen Körper beziehen. Darüber hinaus beschäftigen sich ihre Porträts mit wiederkehrenden Motiven, wie der markanten Nase, der Figur der Mutter oder dem Familienarchiv. Moshtari Hilal is a visual artist and researcher, living in Hamburg and Berlin. In her drawing work Moshtari explores the visual language of the subjective, the hairy and the line. Thus, the artist works with the drawn line as a means and symbol, which refer to the black-haired body. In addition, her portraits deal with recurring motifs, such as the prominent nose, the figure of the mother or the family archive. **www.moshtari.de**

Mit 19 Jahren gelang es **Larissa Bertonasco** ihrem schwäbischen Gefängnis zu entkommen und nach Italien zu fliehen. Da sie dort jedoch schon nach kurzer Zeit in die Gefangenschaft patriarchischer Strukturen geriet, schlug sie sich schließlich gen Norden durch, in die Stadt mit einer Straße namens GROSSE FREIHEIT. Ja, das war endlich der richtige Ort zum Bleiben! Nach der äußeren galt es nun nur noch die innere Freiheit zu erlangen, was sich als ein weitaus schwieriger entpuppte als gedacht. Freiheit empfindet Larissa vor allem beim Meditieren, Tanzen, Singen, Radfahren, Laufen, Sex und beim Zeichnen, zurzeit am liebsten von Lichtprojektionen, zu sehen unter www.bertonasco.de/projektionen At the age of 19, Larissa Bertonasco managed to escape her Swabian prison and flee to Italy. However, after a short time there she found herself captured by patriarchal structures, until she eventually made her way north into the city with a street called GREAT FREEDOM. Yes, this was finally the place to stay! After outer freedom had been achieved, it was now necessary to achieve inner freedom, which turned out to be a lot more difficult than expected. Larissa mostly feels freedom while meditating, dancing, singing, cycling, running, having sex and when drawing – currently, most preferably, drawings of light projections – which can be seen under **www.bertonasco.de/projektionen**

Almuth Ertl – Vor Jahren bin ich aus freien Stücken nach Hamburg gekommen. Ich war so frei, hier zu bleiben und Illustration an der HAW Hamburg zu studieren. Ich bin nicht frei von Zweifeln. Manchmal fühle ich mich frei und manchmal hadere ich mit der Unfreiheit in meinem Leben. Sie haben die Freiheit, mehr von mir zu sehen unter www.almuth-ertl.de Almuth Ertl – Years ago I came to Hamburg of my own free will. I was so free to stay here and study illustration at the HAW Hamburg. I am not free of doubt. Sometimes I feel free and sometimes I struggle with the lack of freedom in my life. You have the freedom to see more of me at **www.almuth-ertl.de**

Karina Tungari kommt aus Jakarta, Indonesien. Zur Zeit ist sie in Hamburg gelandet. Sie findet eine absolute Freiheit existiert nicht. Mehr von Karina: www.karinatungari.com, Instagram @_katung_ Karina Tungari is from Jakarta, Indonesia. She is currently stationed in Hamburg. She finds that absolute freedom does not exist. More from Karina: **www.karinatungari.com, Instagram @_katung_**

Katharina Kulenkampff ist freischaffende Illustratorin. Sie hat Visuelle Kommunikation an der Kunsthochschule Berlin Weißensee studiert. Ihre Arbeiten umfassen handgemachte Bücher, Drucke und kleine Stickereien. Wenn sie nicht zeichnet, druckt oder stickt, genießt sie ihre Freiheit beim Spaziergang im Galgenberg mit ihrem Hund. Katharina Kulenkampff is a freelance illustrator. She studied visual communication at the Berlin Weissensee School of Art. Her work consists of handmade books, prints, and small embroideries. When she is not drawing, printing or embroidering, she enjoys her freedom while walking her dog on Galgenberg (Gallows Hill). **www.kulenkampff.xyz**

Carolin Löbbert hat nach einem Studium an der HAW Hamburg ihre Arbeiten in diversen Gruppen- und Einzelausstellungen gezeigt – unter anderem in Tokio, Antwerpen und Berlin – sowie in Magazinen und Anthologien veröffentlicht. Sie arbeitet in den Bereichen Illustration, Kunst und Grafik für verschiedene internationale Verlage, Agenturen und Labels und hat bereits zwei Bücher veröffentlicht. Carolin Löbbert studied at the HAW Hamburg and, after completing the program, went on to show her work in various groups and solo exhibitions – including in Tokyo, Antwerp and Berlin – as well as in magazines and anthologies. She works in the fields of illustration, art and graphics for various international publishers, agencies and labels and has already published two books. **www.carolinloebbert.de, www.instagram.com/carolinloebbert**

Romy Blümel nimmt sich die Freiheit für SPRING immer mal wieder etwas Neues auszuprobieren. Dieses Jahr versucht sie sich am Cover. Für einen Beitrag im Heft gab es im Lockdown leider zu wenig Freiraum. Romy illustriert für Buch, Zeitung und Bühne mit Farbe, Pinsel und Nadel. Romy Blümel takes the liberty of trying out something new every now and then for SPRING. This year she tried her hand at the cover. Unfortunately, there was not enough free time for an article in the magazine during the lockdown. Romy illustrates books, newspapers, and stages with paint, brush and needle. **www.romybluemel.de**

2021

www.springmagazin.de
Instagram:@springmagazin

© SPRING GbR, Hamburg 2021

Cover: Romy Blümel
Typografie Kapiteltitel: Romy Blümel

Übersetzung: Anita Matkovic, Wien
Lektorat: Nadja Gebhardt, Berlin
Layout und Produktion: Sandra Meifarth, Berlin

Druck: Druckhaus Sportflieger, Berlin
Papier: BIO TOP 3® next

Im Vertrieb des mairisch Verlags
[mairisch 86]
ISBN 978-3-948722-13-5

Alle Rechte vorbehalten.

www.mairisch.de
www.springmagazin.de